# THE TRUTH

## THAT NO ONE TELLS TEENAGERS

Ten Facts Every Teen Victim Has the Right to Know

Matthew McVarish

RAPHAEL PUBLICATIONS

First published by Raphael Publications 2019



ISBN: 978-1-9162475-1-2

Cover design by James Pawson

Cover photograph by Susan Smith

# About the Author

Matthew McVarish is an actor, writer, award-winning human rights activist, and survivor of childhood sexual abuse.

He has appeared on TV, in theatre and film in the UK and worldwide, and written various plays, including:

*To Kill a Kelpie*
*Remember You Are Beauty Full*
*The Child Made of Love*
*Kind Stranger.*

Matthew has chaired international discussions on children's rights at the United Nations and the first Global Survivor Forum for ECPAT International, the largest organisation in the world tackling childhood sexual exploitation.

Go to **www.matthewmcvarish.com** to watch Matthew's TEDx talk: "You actually can".

# This book was written for you.

You have found exactly what you need to know

right now

but

if reading this becomes too much, don't worry.

Just put it down

and come back to it

when you know you're ready.

*You're going to be okay.*

*The truth will set you free, but first it will piss you off.*

—Gloria Steinem

# Contents

# Prologue

## How do I know the truth?

My uncle ruined my childhood. Everyone thought he was such a nice guy, but when we were alone he would do things to me that no one else knew about.

I never told anyone. I believed it was better for everyone if I kept it to myself, but when I became a teenager, I started to feel angry. I felt completely alone.

Sometimes I was okay, really okay in moments, and sometimes I felt nothing at all, like I was numb. Sometimes my thoughts went so fast I believed I would never feel happy again. It was exhausting. A few times I wanted to die.

Twenty years after the abuse, I finally spoke about it. My uncle went to prison. I've now worked all over the world, encouraging people to talk about the abuse they've suffered. To help them begin to heal.

I received a letter from a child who had recently suffered abuse, asking what had helped me recover. As I wrote back, I realised I was telling this child all the things no one told me. The truth I needed to know, back when I was thirteen, that no one around me knew or was willing to tell me.

I had to search for years to find these answers for myself. You have been through enough already; you shouldn't have to search for years like I did. You're about to learn the truth you need to know right now, so you can take back control of the rest of your life.

Recovery is a direction, not a destination. You're either getting better or you're not, and getting back to a good place after what they did to you can take a while. It's so unfair, but if you think about it, the sooner you start this healing the sooner you'll be okay again. So, let's just get on with it.

Recovery happens in three phases:

**Phase 1: Discovering the truth**

**Phase 2: Understanding the truth**

**Phase 3: Believing the truth**

You're nailing Phase 1 right now just by reading this book: well done, you! Phase 2 might happen at the same time, though some truths can be confusing. Take as long as you need. Read this book as many times as you want.

The third and final phase is the simplest and the hardest. It might take years. I know, it's so not fair, but there are ways to speed up this process and the good news is you're starting now. You're beginning your recovery long before I did. Again, well done, you! Think of how many people still don't know the truth or even where to find it. Some people who were abused during their childhood never heal, so the person who ruined their childhood also ruined the rest of their lives. *That will not happen to you.* You're taking control back, just by continuing to read.

I am proud of you for opening this book.

Be brave and read on.

You're going to be okay.

## Remember to breathe

It's simple. We can survive for three weeks without food, for three days without water, but for only three minutes without breathing. It starts the moment we are born and stops the moment we die; breathing is such an automatic process of our bodies that being reminded to do it might seem stupid.

The truth is, we all constantly forget to breathe. Whenever we're scared, excited, or just concentrating on something, we accidentally hold our breath. It's a natural reaction. We unconsciously tense up and stop breathing, even if the stressful situation is just in our imagination – like when we're watching a scary film or reading a good book. We also forget to breathe when we remember something scary from our past or worry about something possibly challenging in the future.

When I was training to become an actor, I was taught, "If in doubt, breathe out" if we were acting on stage and couldn't remember our next line. Instead of panicking, we learned to simply breathe out. It only takes a moment and is often all we need to make our mind shut up for a second.

Taking a nice deep breath is the quickest way to step back from whatever is in your head and instantly relax, like hitting your own personal reset button. If you ever find yourself anxious, scared, or just focusing so hard on something that you get a little lost: *breathe.*

As you read on, I'll regularly remind you to stop and breathe. There is nothing scary here, *no graphic descriptions of abuse*, but

I understand how reviewing memories from my journey, from victim into recovery, might cause you to recall similar memories of your own.

You are safe now. You are reading this to make sense of what you have experienced and to help yourself heal, so be very gentle with yourself and read on at your own pace.

I once flew to Norway to attend a retreat run by Mike Lew, a world-leading specialist in recovering from sexual abuse in childhood. Forty men from all over the world came together to talk about their difficult experiences and help each other to heal. As I nervously approached the large room full of guys just like me, anxious about what we might discuss, yet determined to take back control of our lives, I noticed a sign on the door that simply said:

*Remember to breathe*

Phase 1: Discovering

# The Truth

The Truth is:

# It's not fair

Before I was born, my parents chose my uncle Terry to be my godfather. This meant that he would be the person who would look after me if anything should ever happen to them. Terry, whose real name was Terence, was my mum's younger brother. He worked as a schoolteacher and in his spare time he helped to run a football team of young teenage boys.

Terry was generous, always spoiling his nephews with gifts and sweets. He was kind – volunteering his time for free to help the boys play football. Plus, he was professionally trained to teach children. On top of all that, he was family. To my parents, he seemed like the perfect choice of guardian for their new baby boy.

At my christening, Terry held me up in front of everyone and promised to protect me forever. Then a priest poured holy water over my head and blessed me with the name *Matthew Terence*.

My mum and dad had no idea that the man they'd just named me after was going to abuse me throughout my whole childhood. I can't remember exactly when Terry started abusing me. I guess it must have been while I was too young to even form memories. Thinking back, I just remember always being abused, as if it was a normal part of life, like going to school or helping my mum with the groceries.

I hated everything Terry did to me, but he did it so regularly that, at first, I had no idea it wasn't supposed to be happening at all. He seized every opportunity to get me alone, abusing me in his house, in my house, in my cousin's house, in bedrooms, bathrooms, living rooms, on holiday, in his car… the list goes on and on. Literally nowhere was safe.

My parents didn't stop him because they had no idea what he was doing to me and I didn't know how to tell them. I imagined that if I did say something, my mum would get really upset and my dad would get angry, then perhaps there would be a lot of shouting. I didn't want that. Arguments scared me, so I stayed quiet to keep life peaceful for everyone.

I was a tiny kid who was secretly being used in the most embarrassing way, by the one adult who had sworn to protect me, and I was too scared to tell the only people who I believed could help me because I didn't want to cause any trouble.

It's so easy to see how unfair this was when I look back on it, but the same is true for you right now.

No matter who your abuser was, what they did to you was not fair. It was never okay for them to do anything they did to you. *They* are completely responsible for *their* terrible actions. ALL blame is on them.

It's not fair that the other adults around you allowed it to happen. It's not fair that your childhood was interrupted in this horrible way, and it's so not fair that after everything you've been through already, you are the one left to pick up the pieces and put your life back together. You should not have to go through any of this! It might seem like this first truth is obvious, but to begin to heal, it's really important that you fully grasp this: what you have been through was not fair. It was a massive violation of so many of your human rights. So many other adults, who should have protected you, let you down. They messed up, so badly, and you got hurt. It's not fair!

This should not have been done to you.

But… it was.

The first problem for many people who have experienced abuse is that they cannot accept what was done to them, because it was not fair. Children are not supposed to be abused, *ever*. It's just wrong. So, they burn with anger, insisting that their childhood should not have been that way, but then they get stuck in that rage. As they can't change the past but they also refuse to accept it, every day starts to feel heavy and they start to feel depressed. Eventually, this heavy sadness ruins the rest of their life.

*Don't worry, this will not happen to you.* Just by continuing to read you are gently beginning to save your own life right now.

An awful fact is that what they did to you was actually nothing to do with you. They wanted to do these things to a child, and you were there. If another child had been there, they would have done it to them. It's so incredibly unfair, but it was nothing to do with who you are or what you'd done or what you look like. You were just there.

Stop for a moment right now and just let this sink in. Acknowledge for yourself that you have been treated so unfairly.

**So, now is a good time to take a nice deep breath and breathe out slowly.**

**IN**

**AND**

**OUT**

**Okay, turn the page.**

**Rest your mind on these questions:**

**What is your favourite colour?**

**Why is it your favourite?**

**When did you decide this was your favourite?**

**How does this colour make you feel?**

**Hold on to that feeling as you read on.**

Next, I'll recall how Terry manipulated the people around me. If this reminds you of anything that's uncomfortable at any point just breathe out. Remember, the abuse is not happening now, it's all in the past. However, if you or anyone you know is still being abused, you will find help on what to do at the back of this book.

The Truth is:

**There was nothing you could have done to stop what they did**

One night, when I was around eight years old, I was upstairs in the bath, wasting my dad's shaving foam by giving myself a fluffy Santa Claus beard, when I heard a knock at our front door.

I then heard Terry's voice asking where I was and immediately footsteps coming up the stairs. He had trapped me in the bathroom before, many times, so I leapt out and frantically wrapped a towel around myself. As he reached the bathroom door, I opened it and rushed straight past him.

Watching me hurrying down the stairs dripping water everywhere, Terry picked up another towel and said, "Come back, you haven't dried your hair." I ignored him and went into the living room, where my mum was watching TV. I sat beside her on the couch, hoping I'd be safe this time, but when Terry came back down, he sat right next to me. All I was wearing was a towel.

We used to drape a quilt over the back of the sofa, so I pulled that round me. Even then, my mum had absolutely no idea that I was trying so hard to protect myself from her own brother sitting with us on the couch. She had no reason to suspect anything and he was so relaxed in his constant pursuit of me.

He began making his usual charming chitchat about whatever show was on TV and, as he spoke, he casually put his arm around me. My heart sank but still I never made a noise.

Without even the slightest change in his voice, he kept talking and smiling as he slid his hand under the quilt, then under my towel. He was touching me right in front of my mum, his own sister. She didn't notice. He was a bad man.

I wanted to throw the quilt off and let her see what he was doing, but I didn't. I couldn't. I was too scared. That night, his actions sent a very clear message to me that there really was nothing I could do to stop him.

I remember sitting silently in class the next day. Our teacher was teaching something important, but I wasn't listening. I was just staring at my friend, Simon, wondering if his uncle ever did bad things to him too, or if it was just me. I used to get in trouble a lot for not listening in class. It wasn't fair, I always had a lot on my mind, but I believed I could never tell anyone. I felt so trapped.

The sheer amount of manipulation that Terry worked on my entire family so that he could get me alone, without anyone knowing what he was doing, is astoundingly horrible. He outsmarted countless intelligent adults all around me, including my grandparents, all my aunts and uncles, and even my own mum and dad. I was a child. What chance did I possibly stand of stopping him?

My poor mum had seven kids and I was the youngest. She was always stressed and exhausted with all the cooking, cleaning, and the endless pile of laundry that just regrew every time she finished it.

Whenever Terry would show up offering to take me out for the night, Mum would be relieved –one less noisy kid to deal with for a few hours. She gladly sent me away with him, truly believing that I was safe. Why would she even imagine he would do such terrible things to her child?

Abusers are usually someone the child knows and trusts, and while it is the parents' responsibility to make sure that anyone in contact with their kid is a safe person, I realise that you might be reading this book because you were abused by one of your own parents or stepparents. The point is, no matter who the older, bigger, or stronger person was that abused you, there truly was nothing you could have done to stop them.

Admitting to yourself that you were completely helpless at one time in the past can still feel scary right now, but it does not mean that you are vulnerable anymore. You are much more powerful today. Just look: right now you are taking real, practical steps to reclaim your life. You are already miles ahead of who you were back then. Keep going.

It's natural to keep thinking over everything you experienced and to imagine what you could have said or done differently, but whatever you did or didn't do was the absolute most you could have done at the time. Remember *you were just a child*, and that was an extremely intense situation – one you should not have had to deal with in the first place. If you're still angry with yourself for anything you did or didn't do, forgive yourself, now. It's over. Don't waste another second of your life on it because everything you did was in order to survive. The decisions you made, the actions you did or didn't take, were all your own way of getting through all that stuff. You did the best you could have done in a messed-up, completely unfair situation.

For a moment, right now, just be proud of yourself that you got yourself through it. You are amazing. Really.

**Let's stop and breathe:**

**IN**

**AND**

**OUT**

**Once more?**

**You're doing great.**

**What is your favourite food?**

**Who makes it best?**

**When was the last time you ate it?**

**How does that food make you feel?**

**Hold on to that feeling as you read on.**

Like most challenges in life, it got worse before it got better. As you keep reading, remember it got better. I'm okay now.

You're going to be okay too.

The Truth is:

**You have done nothing wrong**

**They did**

Terry used to shower me with gifts, buying me sweets, toys and sometimes just plainly handing me money. He'd take me on trips in his car and sometimes it was fun. He was easy to talk to and he made me feel very grown up. I accepted everything and never asked why he felt I was so deserving of such special treatment. No one ever seemed to notice his unusual generosity towards me either. He was my godfather and he didn't have any kids of his own, so no one questioned it.

I began to feel guilty, like *I* was using *him* because I knew he would buy me whatever I wanted. All I had to do was keep quiet and let him do whatever he wanted to do to me, then I could have the coolest toys or see the latest movies. My friends were actually jealous of me, but I never felt lucky.

Focusing on the random gifts Terry bought me to make himself feel less guilty for abusing me was just another way I'd discovered to cope with what he was doing to me. I was not agreeing to be abused. I was not selling my body to him for toys. I was not doing anything wrong. I was just trying to look at the situation in any way I could to survive.

On my ninth birthday, Terry arrived with a huge box under his arm – the Lego knight's castle I'd told him to get me. Completely unsurprised as I opened it, I made so little expression of gratitude towards him for this expensive gift that my mum was quite embarrassed. In the kitchen a few moments later, she grabbed me and said sternly, "You should have given your uncle Terry a big hug for buying you that castle."

I stared at her, thinking *Terry will soon take more than a hug for giving me that castle...* but I didn't say anything. I just shrugged and went back through to my party. Mum shook her head and tut-tutted at me, despairing at what an ungrateful child she'd raised.

That night, I was so angry. I locked myself in my sister's room and seethed with frustration. Tears welled in my eyes. I wanted to shout or scream but I knew that if I did, someone might come and make me tell them what was wrong and then I believed I'd be creating a lot of trouble. I sat on the ground in silent despair. The injustice of it all was like hot sick rising up in my throat, though at the same time inside my chest felt complete empty, like a massive cave of nothing.

My face got redder and my fists got tighter. My thoughts began spinning so fast, I didn't know what to do. All this energy surging up in me had to escape somehow, so I started punching myself. Hitting myself in the face, chest, legs, everywhere, but still trying not to make any noise. Just then, I realised I wasn't alone.

Emerging from a deep, cosy sleep, my tabby cat, Jinny, jumped down from the bed to join me on the floor. This innocent little creature had absolutely no idea what I was going through in that moment. Her curious eyes blankly witnessed my torment as I wildly hurled my anger at myself.

Eventually, I fell still. I'm not proud to recall this, but as Jinny came over to show me some love, I sharply pushed her away. Confused, she tried again, manoeuvring round to cuddle into me, but this time I raised my hand and slapped her, hard. I hit her so hard it must have left a bruise under her fur. She shot under the bed and stayed there for the rest of the night.

For twenty years, I felt terrible about hitting Jinny that night, and that wasn't the only time. She was such a sweet little companion;

she never did anything to deserve that. Looking back on it now, as an adult, I can understand why I did it. Hitting my cat was wrong, but I didn't know any better. I was a child who was constantly being hideously abused. My anger at what Terry was doing to me and the fact that I couldn't tell anyone was building pressure like a volcano inside me. It had to escape somehow.

If you've ever hurt yourself, or an animal, or if you ever find yourself wanting to shout at or hurt someone, stop and realise this is just the anger from the abuse that you've suffered escaping. It's good to release that pressure but there are far better ways to do it. Anytime you want, go to the *Help* section at the back of this book to find resources on where you can learn some practical techniques.

It is *never* okay to hurt yourself, or other people or animals, just because you've been hurt by someone else. I used to dream about smashing up Terry's car with a baseball bat, but I knew that was illegal. I didn't want to let him turn me into someone who smashes up cars.

Don't let them change you. Don't let your anger make you hurt yourself or anyone else. You were the victim of their crime.

You have done nothing wrong. They did.

**Time to breathe.**

**You know what to do.**

**Take a nice slow deep breath.**

**It only works if you do it.**

**I trust you.**

**My mum and dad once gave me a Lego train set.
It was my favourite toy of all time.**

**What was your favourite toy when you were little?**

**Can you remember exactly what it looked like?**

**Why was it your favourite?**

**When did you receive it?**

**Where is it now?**

**How does it feel to remember this toy?**

**Take that feeling with you as you read on.**

**Don't forget, you are taking back control of your life as you read on.**

The Truth is:

# It's okay to not be okay

We'd been sitting in his car for around twenty minutes. The windows steamed up from the takeaway food he'd bought us, though it was getting cold now. Terry's house was only five minutes away, but we were just parked up. Silent. I knew something was up. I'd never seen him so lost in thought.

Eventually, he spoke.

"You know when I give you a cuddle?"

I knew he was referring to when he abuses me, but I didn't respond. He continued, "Well, I'm not going to do that anymore."

I couldn't believe it. The thing I'd hoped for all my life had suddenly just happened. Terry was going to stop touching me and I didn't even have to fight him off or tell anyone. This was the happiest moment I'd ever had in my whole life, but all I said was, "Okay."

He looked at me with this deep sadness and added, "But don't tell anyone." He exaggerated this pathetic instruction like he was talking to a four-year-old (though I was eleven). I nodded. He finally started the car and we drove back to his house in silence but inside I was smiling. For the first time in my life I wasn't filled with dread.

He was lying though. Whatever crisis of conscience had led him to try to stop abusing me passed very quickly. He started again and continued, like he always had, for years after that night, when he'd told me he wouldn't do it again.

I started high school feeling devastated. I had always hoped that Terry would have stopped touching me by then. I tried to make new friends, but I always felt outside of the group; like I didn't belong. I believed that if anyone ever found out what my uncle did to me at home, they would never speak to me again.

At home, though inside I felt so sad and alone, I didn't want my parents or siblings to know anything was wrong, so on the outside I kept smiling and laughing. It was like I was becoming two people. When anyone was there, I would act happy, like everything was fine. But when I was alone, I just hated life.

For the first couple years of high school, this was how I lived. My body then began to change and while puberty is a natural process that everyone goes through, it should be experienced in private. Of course, Terry saw my whole body at each stage and would make comments. I would seethe with anger at this cruel invasion of my personal space but, as always, I wouldn't say anything.

Life was an endless task of trying to seem okay, for everyone else's sake. It began to seem like there really was no point in keeping this going. I started imagining killing myself, just to be free.
Whenever I imagined ending my own life, I instantly thought about how upset my family would be and I knew I couldn't do that to them.

It was getting harder and harder to keep up the act. Everything was not okay, so one day, aged twelve, I decided I had to tell someone.

My only teacher who was young and approachable was Mrs McFadden, my maths teacher. I knew that as soon as I told her what had been going on, the reason that I was so lost, everything would change. She'd have to tell my parents and they'd have to tell the police and then all the shouting and the crying that I'd been trying to avoid my whole life would come crashing down around me – all because I'd told someone. But I was scared I might actually kill myself, so it was either tell someone or die.

Walking to her class that morning was like walking towards a bottomless pit that I was going to throw myself into and be falling down forever. I started walking really slowly, trying to slow time. The bell rang and I was still walking. I must have been a couple of minutes late for class, but for me, I was walking towards the end of my life as I knew it.

When I finally walked into the room, Mrs McFadden erupted. I was late for class. That was all she knew. She demanded to know why I was late. I opened my mouth, but with the whole class looking at me, I had no explanation I could easily give. She shouted at me to sit down and, now fizzing with anger, turned away to start the lesson.

I sat down and acted cool, like I didn't care. This seemed to aggravate her even more. I knew I couldn't tell her now; she was so annoyed with me. At the end of the class, when I'd imagined waiting behind to talk to her, I just dashed out, before she could shout at me again. For the rest of my years at high school, I never felt brave enough to try telling anyone again.

Surrounded by friends and family I always felt completely alone, but all those years could have been so different. All that suffering could have been avoided if I'd only *told someone* what was going on – if I'd let someone see that I was not okay, or if I'd been brave enough to not be okay in front of someone. If I could go back in time and talk to myself in high school, there is so much I would say. There is so much I needed to know but no one told me. I can't go back and help my younger self, but I can help you now, today, by telling you everything I wish I'd known.

The truth is, it's totally okay to not be okay. When you let yourself feel whatever you are hiding inside, people can help you. The abuse will stop. I can't promise you that the first person you tell will know what to say, but if they don't, just tell someone else. Keep telling people until you get the help you need. Safe contacts are listed in the *Help* section at the back of this book.

For right now, give yourself a break.

Too many people who have been abused end up throwing the rest of their life away. They try to ignore what they feel inside but then the pressure just builds up. To avoid this pressure, they start to drink too much alcohol or take drugs. Sometimes they become violent or start committing crimes. Some end up homeless. Some even give up on everything and they actually do kill themselves. These tragic outcomes are not inevitable; *these horrible things won't happen to you*. Those poor people just never found the help they needed. They never learned the truth.

Your future can be awesome because, remember, right now you are taking powerful steps to take back control of your life. All the heavy stuff you've lived through is already more difficult than anything about 80% of the population will ever experience. You have not only survived, but right now you are on a self-led mission to make your life better. Think about this for a moment. You are so strong, you've proved that, but it's okay not to be okay all the time. Most people are scared to cry, but crying is our body's natural pressure release. Put on a cosy hoody, find a private place, play some chilled music, and let your tears flow. You won't cry forever, and you will feel better after a good cry.

You really are going to be okay, but it's okay not to be okay for now.

**As slowly as you can, breathe:**

**IN**

**AND**

**OUT**

**IN**

**AND**

**OUT**

**IN**

**AND**

**OUT**

**What is your favourite song?**

**Is it a happy or a sad song?**

**When did you last listen to it?**

**How does hearing it make you feel?**

**Hold on to that feeling.**

In these next memories, I recount when the abuse finally stopped. Don't worry, I don't describe the abuse, just what happened after.

You are doing so well.

You're miles ahead of where I was at your age.

The Truth is:

# None of this is your fault

March twenty-fourth, 1996, 3:56pm, trapped on Terry's bed again, I said I needed to go to the bathroom and then pulled my clothes back on.

Locking the door, I looked out of the window. It was too high. I would break my legs if I jumped out. Then I'd have to explain to people why I'd leapt out of my uncle's third-floor bathroom window.

I was thirteen now and getting quite tall, not the tiny infant I'd been when Terry first started touching me. I'd been really trying to avoid getting stuck alone with him and he'd not been able to touch me as much as when I was little. This time, he'd promised me that my other uncle would be here. Terry wouldn't abuse me if his brother was with us, but he wasn't.

I went into the living room and looked down to the street to see if my other uncle was close. Terry came in behind me, blocking the doorway. I was about eight miles from my own house. If I ran out, I'd need to get a bus home, but I had no money. I noticed a bowl of coins with enough to get me home. I hadn't planned this, but I suddenly pointed at the gas heater and said,

"Your fire is still on!"

As Terry went over to see what I was pointing at, I grabbed a fistful of coins and ran.

Of course, he had locked his front door, so I didn't get far before he grabbed me. Dragging me back into his living room, we were both in shock.

I was terrified but silent. Terry was clearly freaked out, wide-eyed and breathing heavily. For the first time in my life I had tried to save myself. I'd done something other than just let it happen. I had no idea what would happen now.

Terry began to cry saying, "I only do those things because I love you!"

This was crazy talk, but he was just saying anything to make himself feel better. He never loved me. He never even cared about me. He just used me.

Terry drove me home in that odd silence, but without words we both knew he would never be able to abuse me again.

I took a long walk that night, alone. Feeling so many things all at once, I had to clear my head. The coins I'd grabbed earlier were still in my pocket, so I bought some chewing gum and sat on the steps of our local community hall by myself, chewing and thinking.

I knew deep down, although no one had ever told me, that all those years of being abused had seriously hurt me. I knew it could all come back to haunt me when I grew up if I didn't heal from it. There, on those steps, I made a solemn promise to myself that I would never let what Terry had done ruin my future. Without realising it, I'd just made the most powerful decision of my life. I'd decided to heal. The only problem was, I didn't know how.

The abuse had finally stopped, but as no one knew it had been going on to begin with, I had to keep on pretending everything was fine. Terry still came to our house sometimes and I couldn't let anyone realise anything had changed. I never spoke to him again, but I acted so okay whenever he was there that no one even noticed. Life was constant stress, but I had mastered how to hide my feelings and keep the peace.

At home, just acting normal was intense, but on the surface all seemed calm. At school, I made some new friends and even started going out with my first girlfriend, Cara. I wasn't happy, but I was managing to get by. Then I saw a movie called *Good Will Hunting.*

Matt Damon plays Will, a young mathematical genius born into a poor neighbourhood. Despite his academic brilliance, he starts fights in bars and gets arrested all the time. To avoid being sent to prison, Will agrees with the judge that he'll go to therapy to discuss his violence problem. Robin Williams plays Sean, his therapist, tasked with figuring out why Will is so angry all the time.

At first, he is completely silent, refusing to talk about anything, proving to Sean that he can't make him talk about anything if he doesn't want to.

Sean doesn't force him at all, he just waits and waits. Eventually, Will opens up and talks about general things, nothing too deep. It seems Will is a robust character, like he's always fine and nothing ever upsets him. Then, in one surprising scene, Sean looks at Will's case history and sees the long list of horrible abuse Will suffered as a child. All Sean says about it is, "It's not your fault."

Will says, "I know."

Then Sean says it again, "It's not your fault."

Again, Will shrugs it off with, "I know!"

Sean continues, "It's not your fault. It's not your fault. It's not your fault."

As he repeats it calmly, again and again, Sean begins to tap into some deeply held belief within Will and he suddenly begins to cry. This solid guy, who always acts okay, finally cracks.

This scene scared me – the idea that some stranger could make me cry just by telling me the abuse wasn't my fault. Like Will, I knew what Terry did to me was not my fault. I knew that and I understood it. I was only a child and he was a fully-grown man, so I'd completed phases one and two.

In the movie, Will entered phase three: believing the truth. Sean helped him fully realise in his heart that nothing he had endured was his fault. Will was overwhelmed by the relief that he could now finally stop acting like he was always fine and admit everything was not okay.

At that time, I believed crying was a sign of weakness and I was terrified of being vulnerable. I didn't want to lose control of my emotions… ever. Maybe because Terry had made me feel things that I didn't want to feel, I'd decided to become like stone. I would never let myself feel anything that I didn't want to.

As you reflect on everything you've endured, realise right now that you were the victim of a serious crime. You were only a child. They were completely responsible for what they did to you and all the stress it put on you. Absolutely none of this is or ever was your fault.

You might read this and think, *No, I shouldn't have...* or *I could have...* or *If only I had...*

No. These thoughts are just wrong. Stop it. If you honestly believe any of this was even a tiny bit your fault, then the awful truth is that the person who did this to you *also* made you think it was your fault. How incredibly unfair is that? Part of you may want to believe it was your fault because if you believe you were responsible then you can convince yourself that you had some power to stop what they did, but again, there was nothing you could have done to stop them.

As you get older, look at kids who are the age you were when that person first abused you. You will see that this is the truth. The older you get, the easier it is to finally believe this truth, but it is still true right now. You are as innocent right now as you always were.

None of this is your fault.

**Still breathing?**

**Take three breaths as slowly as you can and imagine your chest becoming lighter with each breath.**

**Don't turn this page until you've actually done it.**

**What's your all-time favourite film?**

**What do you love about it?**

**Are the characters in it like you in any way?**

**How did you feel when you first saw it?**

**Hold on to that feeling.**

My story now moves on to my path towards healing, but it wasn't all plain sailing…

The Truth is:

# Talking about it helps

Cara and I had been together for a couple of years and everything seemed to be going fine. We laughed a lot and I just loved being with her. Whenever we were together, I totally forgot about all the stress at home, but around that time some of our friends were turning sixteen and beginning to have sex. I started to feel pressure to become more intimate with Cara. I knew she cared about me and that she wouldn't hurt me, and although I wanted to get closer to her, the idea of being touched again, by anyone, made me shiver.

Despite my fear, we began to try stuff. As usual, I stayed calm on the surface while inside I was terrified. It was stressful, but I didn't let it show. Secretly, I would get angry with myself for not being able to just relax. All my friends seemed to love sex; I didn't want to feel different anymore. I thought that if I didn't like it, then that must be because Terry had damaged me, and I hated that. I didn't want to let him take this away from me too, so I stayed quiet and I kept trying.

Not long after we'd begun being more intimate, I broke up with Cara. I couldn't tell her why. I loved her and I loved being her boyfriend, but it was all getting too much.

Life in my busy house went on as normal, Terry dropped in on occasion and I acted as if everything was fine. At school, I smiled when anyone looked at me and laughed when anyone made a joke.

One night, I found out that my brother Martin was in hospital. I assumed he must have been in some kind of accident, but when my dad and I went to visit him, he was sitting up in the bed completely fine. He didn't look sick or injured. When he spoke, I realised he was ill.

Martin was talking, but he wasn't making any sense, like his mind was so tired that it couldn't keep up with reality anymore. He was ten years older than me and at university. He had been under a lot of additional stress with the course work and suddenly he had collapsed. I had no idea you could become this ill from stress. My dad looked worried, but I was scared. Martin, my big brother, was so lost and confused and I didn't know how to help him.

The doctors gave him some pills to help his mind slow down and he became calm. He could still walk, so we took him out on a little stroll around the hospital grounds for fresh air. As we led him back to the ward, Martin stopped, looked at my dad and said, "I need to tell you something."

My dad looked anxious.

Martin continued, "I was abused by Terry."

As I heard those words, I felt faint. I stayed standing but inside it was like my head exploded. Terry had abused my big brother *too*? All those years I'd believed it had just been me. What did this all mean?

Just like me, Martin had never told anyone. He had been trying to act happy and keep the peace since Terry started abusing him when he was little, but Martin had been holding it together for ten years longer than I had. The end result was that, aged only twenty-five, his mind couldn't cope anymore. He suffered a complete emotional collapse.

Witnessing my big brother, who had always seemed such a happy, robust character, reduced to this vulnerable confused state petrified me. I knew instantly that if I didn't get help, I would end up in a hospital bed in ten years.

Martin stayed in hospital for a few weeks, just resting his mind, but now the truth about what Terry had done to him had been spoken, and I wondered when he would speak to the police.

It didn't happen. This was 1998 and very few abuse victims would actually go to the police. By listening through doors and overhearing phone calls, I soon learned that Terry had also abused two more of our brothers. I couldn't believe how much abuse had been going on, but no one was saying anything.

At home, life became even more intense. I kept on acting happy but now I knew that everyone else was just acting happy too. No one was talking about the difficult truth that we all now knew. The one blessing was that my dad never let Terry back into our home. I didn't have to see him anymore or pretend to like him ever again.

Years passed in silence. I was mentally exhausted. I didn't know how to find help, but I knew that if I didn't start talking about it all soon, I was at risk of getting ill.

My parents were good people, but they didn't know how to deal with any of this either. Many parents don't. They hoped that time would heal, and so we just carried on, waiting for better times. I knew that wasn't going to work.

I turned seventeen and applied for any job as far away from home as I could find. One month after completing high school, I got on a train and moved three hundred miles away. I'd landed a position working for a Youth Theatre for under-privileged children in

Wolverhampton. Leaving home was scary but staying at home for any longer was scarier.

In my first week at my new job, we took all the kids to the theatre to see *Westside Story*. After the show, we dropped them all at home and my new colleague, Rachel, asked if I wanted to go out for some food. It was quite late but the Indian restaurants in Wolverhampton stay open very late. Rachel was a little older than me and had already been working with teenagers for a few years. That night, without expecting to at all, I told her everything. I could barely look at her as I spoke but, after more than a decade of silence, I'd finally told someone what I'd been through.

Rachel wasn't shocked or freaked out at all. She just listened. Then, when I'd finished, she told me I should be proud of myself for having survived all that. She gave the phone number of a special place called Base 25 that gave free therapy to teenagers, then she looked into my eyes and told me that I was going to be okay. I'd never had anyone who really understood what I was dealing with, say that to me before. I felt weirdly lighter; like I'd finally put down a bag of bricks I'd been carrying for years.

This is how I started therapy at age seventeen, only four years after my abuse had stopped. It wasn't fun; it wasn't easy; but I knew that if I kept going, I was saving my own life. Like chemotherapy for cancer patients, it's uncomfortable, but it's healing you.

You don't ever have to talk about the scary details of what they did to you. Just talk about your feelings; how you feel right now, how you felt back then, and how you feel about the future.

Talking with someone safe about these things is like slowly and gently letting the pressure out of a bottle of Coke that's been shaken up. You get to stay in control of releasing all the hurt and pain. Not talking about how you feel means that the pressure just builds up. It doesn't go away and eventually bursts out in other ways – ways you don't want; ways you can't control.

A lot of people who have been abused never talk about it, and they often end up smoking, compulsively overeating, taking drugs, or drinking too much alcohol. These are all just ways of numbing themselves from all that pressure, but smoking makes them stink and ill, junk food makes them overweight and ill, drugs make them weird and ill and alcohol makes them lose control and become ill. All these things eventually ruin their health and they all die younger. Remember, these things do not have to happen.

Talking about it helps, but there are a lot of different kinds of therapy, not just talking, and there are a lot of people just waiting to help you. See the back of this book.

You are already saving your own life, right now. You ARE going to be okay.

**Breathe in slowly like your body is a bucket you're trying to fill with air, from the bottom up.**

**Breathe out slowly like gently pouring the air back out.**

**Really, try it. You'll feel better.**

**If you could live anywhere in the whole world, where would you choose?**

**If money wasn't an obstacle, would you prefer an apartment in New York or a quiet country villa in Italy, or a bamboo hut on a tropical beach?**

**What does your ideal future home look like?**

**Describe it to yourself and imagine making everything in it exactly the way you want it.**

**Now imagine you already live there.**

**Feel how good it would feel.**

**Hold on to this feeling.**

**How are you doing?**

**Remember that you can put this book down at any point and come back to it.**

**Be brave.**

The Truth is:

# Your whole life is not ruined

I stayed in Wolverhampton for another two years and continued therapy. Even though sometimes I felt sad or angry afterwards, I learned to just let my feelings show. Rachel was good at helping me let my emotions out instead of burying them again. I noticed that once you let yourself feel something you've been trying to avoid, it just goes away, but if you try to push it down, it just gets stronger.

Everything I told my therapist was true, except my name. I said my name was Ryan. I liked that name and I was scared that if I gave them my real name, they'd call the police about Terry. Then I'd have created that whole scary courtroom drama that I now knew my family was trying to avoid. And I never told my therapist about my dreams. I kept them to myself.

Each day I felt more and more like I was taking back control of my life and I even began setting goals for my future. I'd always wanted to become an actor, so I applied to some acting courses and was accepted by a university in Edinburgh. This meant moving back up to Scotland, but I'd be on the other side of the country from everyone I knew.

Cara and I met up again and after all those years apart we got back together. As I turned nineteen, it seemed that life was finally getting better.

Cara and I became intimate again and although I still found it stressful, this time I told her about everything Terry had done to me. She was very patient and understanding. I felt safe and loved.

Drama school was another intense environment. There was so much to learn and, unfortunately, real acting involves allowing yourself to be vulnerable – the thing I'd spent most of my life trying to avoid. I soon made new friends and forgot about therapy, but I had no idea what was about to happen.

One night, a guy in my acting class told me he was gay. This was quite a surprise because he had always insisted that he liked girls. I asked him how he had lived so long without knowing he was gay and he said that whenever he found himself thinking about another guy, he would just chase the thought out of his mind, never allowing himself to have a "gay thought".

When he said this, the walls of my whole world fell down. I'd never told my therapist but sometimes when I was asleep, I had dreams about guys. When I was awake, I would never let myself think any "gay thoughts". I was sure that Terry abusing me from such a young age had somehow messed up my brain, because even though I hated everything he did to me, some of it made my body feel kind of nice. I was so disgusted with myself about this and I was worried it had caused these random dreams about men. I hoped that one day, when I was brave enough, I would find the right therapist to help me get rid of those confusing dreams, but when my friend described how he had been editing his thoughts, I realised I'd been doing the same thing.

In that instant I realised that I was not "messed up", I was actually just gay. There's nothing wrong with being gay, but I was in shock. How had I not realised this truth all my life?

To be very clear, being abused by Terry had *not* turned me gay. That cannot happen. He also abused three of my brothers and they all have wives and children now. I was born gay but being abused by a man throughout my entire childhood meant I was so scared of sex that I never allowed myself to think about it long enough to realise I was gay.

No one can change your sexual preference. We are born straight or gay or whatever and nothing can change that. The problem for many people who have been abused is that it can take longer to figure out what orientation they have, because of all the pain and fear associated with sex.

In some parts of the world, groups of horrible men go around sexually assaulting any women who identify as lesbian, because they stupidly believe that it will "cure" them. This is utterly crazy and so wrong. You cannot alter anyone's sexual orientation by sexually traumatizing them.

Whoever abused you has not changed you either. You are still the awesome person inside that you were always going to be, before the abuse you suffered. No matter if you're straight or gay or bi or whatever, be proud of who you are.

If you're not sure what you are yet, take your time. You don't need to rush into anything. Remember, talking about it with someone safe helps.

When I realised I was gay, I had to tell Cara. She was as surprised as me, but we soon became just good friends. I then went straight back to therapy. I couldn't believe I had to go back but my mind was all mixed up again and I needed someone to help me figure everything out.

Most talk-therapy is just sitting in a cosy room across from a kind, patient person who just listens to you talking. You can decide what you want to talk about and they don't ask you any difficult questions. They're just there to help you get clear on everything in your head, like taking everything out of a cupboard, organising it and putting the useful things back in again. Talking to this safe person is just like taking the thoughts out your head, deciding if you want to keep them or throw them away. Soon, your mind becomes more organised inside, so it gets easier to think and feel happy.

Going to therapy once doesn't mean you're "fixed" forever. You might go every week for a few months and then, when you feel better, quit. Years later, something new might happen to make you feel overwhelmed again, so you go back.

Our mind is kind of like a musical instrument in this way. You need to tune the strings on a guitar before you can play it, but then after a while you need to tune them back up again.

Occasionally, we all need someone to help us talk through our problems and there's no shame in asking for help. If you broke your leg, you would go straight to hospital. In a few months it will have healed. Mental health is the same. If you ever feel overwhelmed, go and find a therapist. You'll soon be feeling like yourself again.

I'll never forget watching the *Oprah Winfrey Show* when she interviewed a convicted child sex-offender. She asked him what he thought he had done to that little girl, who was now grown up and struggling with depression. He said, "I murdered the person she could have been."

This is the way he saw it, but the girl he abused was still alive; her future was still unwritten.

What your abuser did to you might have ruined your childhood, but what happens next is up to you. You can choose to heal your emotional wounds.

It can seem too big at first, but you will get there. Remember, everyone is responsible for their own life. If you want a big house or a nice car, only you can make it happen, no one will come along and give you these things. This is also true of overcoming your traumatic past. YOU must take control.

Like I did, decide right now that whatever that horrible person did to you will not take away the beautiful future you have ahead of you. Decide now.

Lots of successful people were abused in childhood and didn't let their life slip away; the difference is that they made the decision and chose to pursue healing. And success doesn't just mean having lots of money. It means being genuinely happy. You deserve that.

Your whole life is not ruined. You have the power to make the rest of it awesome.

Time to breathe.

Take three slow breaths but this time imagine you're breathing in through your eyes. Then slowly breathe out through your ears.

IN

AND

OUT

Weirdly relaxing, huh?

Two more times…

Well done you.

**Remember, no one can hear your thoughts.**

**Honestly, what celebrity do you like the most?**

**It's okay, this is totally private, only for you.**

**What is it about them that you like so much?**

**Now, imagine meeting them.**

**How does that thought make you feel?**

**Hang on to this feeling.**

**There will be twists and turns on the road to recovery. The main thing is to keep going.**

The Truth is:

**You will be stronger because of what you have lived through**

University is a stressful time for everyone, but on top of all the course work, I was now trying to figure out who I was. Having recently discovered I was gay, which meant I lost my relationship with Cara, I was quite insecure and feeling vulnerable again. I didn't share what was going on with my classmates yet because I didn't think they would understand. Even at parties, I would go off on my own to find a quiet place to think.

At one party, a guy I didn't know came into the kitchen and started asking me what was up. Maybe I was a little too drunk, or maybe I was too tired of trying to cope with everything by myself, but I decided to tell him what I was going through. He listened and he gave me another drink. He seemed nice. I didn't realise that he was not a safe person. That guy drugged me.
The next morning, I woke up and discovered that I'd been abused again. I was twenty years old.

This obviously set me back a long way in my healing. It meant that it would take me a lot longer before I felt safe enough to begin any kind of gay relationship. I started having nightmares again and flashbacks. I would often zone out whenever I was in class because something someone said would send my mind rambling over everything I'd suffered. I was very unwell. Luckily, by then I knew that trauma of this kind requires therapy, so I went back… again. I learned new practical techniques like Tapping. Simply tapping your fingers on your hands or face stops your mind racing and returns you to a calm state in the present moment. (Find more information in the *Help* section). Opening up to friends also helped and asking my university to give me a little less work to do while I got my head together was a huge help. It meant telling them what had happened, but I was telling the truth and I'd done nothing wrong. I had nothing to be ashamed of.

If I hadn't asked for all that help straight away, I wouldn't have been able to get well enough to finish university, then I would have let the person who had abused me ruin my whole career. I might have even ended up in hospital, too stressed to think, but by being brave and talking through it all with a professional, I was able to get my life back on track.

I graduated with a degree in acting, signed with a big London agent and immediately started working in theatre and on TV. I wasn't letting my past trauma win; I was making my dreams come true.

After a few years of acting in plays, I started writing them too. Life was better than it had ever been but one day I got a call from my brother's wife. Not Martin's wife, my other brother, Francis.

He was also abused by Terry and had never really talked about it. His wife told me that he too was now becoming overwhelmed with stress. I kind of knew this might happen and although I wasn't happy about it, I also wasn't surprised.

I went to visit him and we tried to talk, but it was hard. These are very uncomfortable memories for two brothers to discuss together. Instead, we chose to avoid our feelings, went to a bar and got drunk. We staggered back to his house in the middle of the night. It was so dark we couldn't see each other's faces. So, standing outside, smoking and looking up at the stars, we finally began talking.

I'd been in and out of therapy for eight years at this point, but this was just the beginning of his healing.

I came home full of rage and sadness all over again, but this time I was feeling it on his behalf. I was so angry that my brother was so stressed, that all my brothers had to go through this when it was Terry who created it. He should be the one suffering.

I hadn't seen Terry in years, but I knew he was still registered as a schoolteacher. I had no idea if he was abusing boys in the school, but I did know he was a dangerous child sex-offender who, so far, had abused three of my brothers and me. Why couldn't we talk about that? Why did we need to get so drunk and wait until the middle of the night before we could even broach the subject, when none of it was even our fault?

I'd had enough. I knew I wasn't going to stay quiet any longer, but I didn't want to run straight to the police. Martin, Francis, and our other brother, Patrick, were all at different stages of their own healing and I imagined that taking Terry to court would create a lot of added stress. I didn't want to force them to do that if they weren't ready for it. We all just needed to talk to each other, but I didn't know how to make that happen.

As I was now writing theatre professionally, I decided to write a play called *To Kill a Kelpie*, about brothers who had suffered abuse in their childhood who finally come together to talk about it.

A "Kelpie" is a mythological Scottish monster. It would appear at the side of a loch as a charming man, but when children got close it would grab them and drown them in the water. This seemed like the perfect metaphor for a child sex-offender.

The play features twin brothers who were both abused by the same uncle, but as they grow up, one goes to therapy and the other never speaks about it at all. As you might expect, the one who went to therapy is now in touch with his emotions, moving on with his life, discovering new things about himself and making good progress. The other is still acting fine, although inside he keeps everything locked down. This eventually leads him to have a total meltdown, just as I'd witnessed in real life.

The play was produced within a year and I invited my brothers to come to see it. I knew it would be hard for them to watch, so I invited help.

Sandra Brown, OBE, founder of The Moira Anderson Foundation that supports victims and survivors of childhood sexual abuse, came to the theatre and led a discussion after my show.

After twenty years of staying quiet, acting happy and ignoring the fact that Terry was still in contact with children, my brothers and I finally came together and spoke the truth with each other. Sandra herself contacted the police for us and the staff of her foundation supported us all through the whole legal process.

Within just a few weeks of my play, Terry was arrested. He was tried in court and sent to prison for everything that he did to us. He lost, we won.

The court case wasn't a joyful experience. From the day the police took my statement to the day Terry was sent to prison it took nearly two years, but we only went to court a couple of times. He pleaded guilty, which meant that we didn't have to speak in court. Your abuser might try to pretend they were innocent, so if you are asked to speak in court, understand that there are new special arrangements to make the experience as stress-free as possible for you. There are many organisations, like The Moira Anderson Foundation, all over the world waiting to help you through all this. You'll be okay. Be brave, remember to breathe, and be proud that you are speaking the truth. The process will be handled for you by the police and court officials, but it's okay to ask as many questions as you want, whenever you want. You will be able to handle it. You've survived worse already. The abuse itself is in the past, so the court case is basically just words.

Giving the police a statement is really, really boring, because they have to write every single sentence very slowly to be sure it's accurate. But to help the court reach the best possible outcome for you, it's important that you tell the police everything you can remember in the statement. If it's scary, remember you are doing it to take your life back and it will be over soon.

Now Terry was in prison and my brothers and I were all on our own healing journeys, but we were no longer struggling in isolation. We could lean on each other for support.

Looking back, I wish we had done this sooner, but when I was young the police really weren't great at handling these kinds of crimes.

Thankfully, there have been a lot of improvements in the last twenty years. I'm not saying it's easy and I wish you didn't have to go through this at all, but if the person who abused you is still in contact with children, then you could literally save lives by reporting them.

It is not your fault if they abuse more children. You are not responsible for their actions. The police need to stop them, but they can't do anything until a victim comes forward. After suffering the abuse itself, victims are often too scared to ever face their abuser again. Abusers know that. So they get away with it.

You might think you're not strong enough to go through all this, but realise that you are stronger than the child they might abuse tonight, or tomorrow, or next year, until you say something. You'll become stronger. If you fall and break your leg, your body heals the break by slowly adding extra layers of bone over the crack. After you recover, your leg actually ends up stronger than it was before it was broken. Our mind is the same. Because you have been through all these tough experiences, when you're older you will be much stronger emotionally than people who have never lived through anything difficult. You will be kinder because you understand what real pain feels like. Our world really needs more strong, kind people.

You could choose to ignore what they did to you, never talk about it, never report them, and just drown your feelings in alcohol, drugs, or being violent towards other people who don't deserve it. But throwing the rest of your life away is simply letting that person win, the one who ruined your childhood.

Do not ever let them win.

**Try this:**

**Imagine you have nostrils on your lower back.**

**Breathe in slowly, filling up from the bottom of your spine to the top.**

**And, again.**

**Once more.**

**Can you feel a difference once you've done it?**

**What is your dream job?**

**What would you love to be paid to do?**
**(Eating and watching Netflix doesn't count...)**

**What is it about this job that you love?**

**Now, imagine it's the future and you already have this job. Think back over the past few years to where you are now and imagine the steps you took to get this job.**

**It is possible.**

**How does your dream job make you feel?**

**Hold on to this feeling.**

**You can do this.**

The Truth is:

# You have nothing to be ashamed of

Terry was in prison and my brothers and I were talking openly with each other about our past.

After witnessing how my play *To Kill a Kelpie* had catalysed such a positive change in my family, I realised it could probably do the same for others. Soon, there were more productions of it, not just in the UK but across the USA too. Survivors from near and far would tell me how the play had inspired them to get help and, for the first time, speak to their families or a therapist or the police.

I then started to speak out publicly about what Terry had done to me and the more I did, the more people came up to me and said they'd been abused too. It was astounding at first, but I soon realised there are hundreds of millions of people across the world that have endured this.

You might have felt alone for a long time, or like no one understands how you feel, but I had no idea that three of my own brothers were going through exactly the same things I was – feeling alone but standing right next to each other. What you and I have experienced is actually the same as about every fifth child in the world.

Think of all the other kids in your school. Now realise that up to 30% of them will have experienced abuse by the age of eighteen. They probably feel as alone as you have in the past.

After a while, working on my play was feeling too heavy, so I decided to make a film version of it. That way it could reach more people. My brother Martin happens to be an award-winning filmmaker now, so he directed and produced it. Francis helped us build the set and Patrick did the catering for the film shoot.

We were working together on a film inspired by our past trauma; a film that we knew would help so many more people out there who still needed to find the courage to speak out.

Thankfully, the film seems to have the same effect on audiences as the play. People who watch it tell me how it has helped them decide to get help, so I wanted to show the film to as many people as possible. I imagined screenings of it in loads of different countries, but I wasn't sure how to do that. Eventually I came up with a very ambitious plan.

It seemed like a crazy idea at first, but I decided to take a few of years out of my acting career to walk 10,000 miles. It took a lot of preparation. First, I learned how to meditate, which meant I was equipped to cope with the stress of walking twelve hours a day for nearly two years, then five organisations collaborated internationally to help me create the project, including The Moira Anderson Foundation.

I left London on foot and over the course of nearly two years, I visited thirty-two nations, showing the film and speaking to the press to increase awareness of child sexual abuse. I took around forty-eight million steps, but this meant I was on TV, radio, and newspapers. My words were translated into over thirty languages, encouraging millions of survivors to talk about the abuse they'd suffered.

I soon learned that some countries had a law that actually stops victims from pressing charges. There's a time limit on reporting, so many survivors who finally feel ready to speak to the police are told they've missed their chance. Then the person who abused them is free and can't even be arrested.

So, as I reached each country, I asked their government to remove this dangerous law. Some parliaments took action immediately. I was then invited to meet the Pope.

I prepared to tell him about my walk and all the reasons we need to change the laws, but when I met him the first thing I said was, "Papa, my uncle abused me."

I wasn't even Catholic anymore. Saying all those prayers as a kid while knowing they weren't actually saving me from Terry meant I'd lost my respect for religion long ago, but despite that, I still believed in God. It's okay if you don't, but many people do. I don't imagine God as some wise old man with a long white beard sitting up in the clouds. My dad taught me that God is love. Do you believe in love? It's easy to understand why someone who has experienced what we have might not, but despite the loveless treatment we have endured, love does exist. Sometimes, when things were really tough, like walking thirty miles every day through the rain with no money to eat, in my head I'd ask God for help. Help always came, one way or another, although I never heard God speak back to me directly. For many people around the world, the Pope is the one person on Earth who represents God. He speaks for him. So, when he looked me in the eye and put his hands on my head, I felt that, on behalf of God, he was genuinely sorry that this had been done to me. It was quite a moment.

I wish everyone who has suffered abuse could experience this. Even if you don't believe in God, having the person who represents Him personally acknowledge all that you've suffered is profoundly validating.

After making it home safely, I was invited back to speak to all forty-seven nations of Europe. I flew to Strasbourg and requested that all governments in Europe uphold the rights of their own citizens by abolishing their limit on reporting child sexual abuse. I was now encouraging positive change over a territory of eight hundred and twenty million people. It was quite a journey, one which I never imagined I'd end up on when I first wrote the play to encourage my brothers and I to talk.

While I was visiting all those countries, I started to notice something. No one anywhere is comfortable talking about abuse, but the reasons they don't like to talk about it are different.

Whenever I met a survivor, I always asked them the same question, "Why didn't you tell anyone?" They always gave the same answer – they felt ashamed.

I began to discover that shame is literally geographical. If you have an ear infection and a broken arm you feel pain, but they're different kinds of pain. To heal those two problems requires very different treatment. There are also different kinds of shame and each victim's shame depends on things such as what religion their family is (if any), if there has been any war around them, or how progressive their community is on LGBTQ+ issues or gender equity.

You can't control these things, but they can directly influence how long it will take you to feel ready to report the abuse, if ever. Imagine these three victims who all live in the same country right now: an eight-year-old Catholic boy from a poor family, a teenage Muslim girl in a wealthy family, and a trans child growing up on a small island off the coast. These three kids live in the same country, but they occupy very different worlds.

Look around you. What is it about your environment that makes you feel you can't tell people what you've been through? Then realise that those things are not stopping you – you are. New Age thinker, Geoff Thompson said, "It's not obstacles that keep us stuck but the fact that we have not overcome them."

If you ever feel shame about what you've suffered, imagine a little kid playing outside in the garden when a drunk driver suddenly veers off the road into the garden and hits them. Do you think the child should feel ashamed? Do you think it was the kid's fault they got hit? Do you think victims of a car crash should never tell anyone about it? Would you feel ashamed of being the victim of that car crash? Obviously, the person driving the car was completely responsible for the terrible thing they did and the pain it caused the victim. The kid hit by the car was not to blame and has nothing to be ashamed of. Somehow, because abuse involves parts of our bodies that we are usually embarrassed to talk about, this truth is not as obvious, but it's still true:

*You have nothing to be ashamed of.*

**You're almost through Phase 1!**

**Celebrate with a huge deep breath.**

**IN**

**AND**

**OUT**

**If you could have a new skill, what would you choose?**

**It could be anything: speaking another language, meditation, mountain climbing, carpentry, playing an instrument, being an excellent conversationalist… anything.**

**What would you do with this skill?**

**How would feel if you were a master of it?**

**You know, you can actually do that.**

**If you start now, in a few months you'll be there.**

**This final truth is the most important of all.**

The Truth is:

**You are awesome and the world needs you**

This is probably the hardest truth to believe, but still totally true. You deserve the best in life.

The most heart-breaking part of working with abuse survivors from all over the world is meeting all these awesome people who have absolutely no idea that they are awesome, all because of what some disgusting person did to them a long time ago.

Awesome doesn't just mean "really good", like it seems to these days. The word actually means awe-inspiring. Like WOW!

Every single child is capable of incredible things. Whatever happened to you hasn't changed that.

You don't have to go around telling people how awesome you are, but you do need to understand and believe it for yourself, quietly in your heart. Imagine one person who knows they are awesome and another person who doesn't. Their lives will look very different.

When you don't know that you're awesome you don't strive to give yourself the awesome things in life that you deserve. You might end up in a relationship with someone who doesn't respect you and it might take a few years of putting up with their unfair treatment before you finally understand that you deserve better. If you already knew that you deserved better, you wouldn't have gotten into that relationship to begin with. When you know you deserve better, you work hard to make the world around you better. Now, imagine a world full of people who understand how awesome they are. Our world really needs more people like that.

After my address to all forty-seven governments in Europe, I was invited by the United Nations to chair a discussion, where delegates representing entire continents came together to talk about positive change. I was now in charge of a global discussion. Then, while I was working for the UN, I was invited to Asia, to work for ECPAT International. They are the biggest organisation tackling sexual violations of children in the whole world, with projects in over ninety countries. They asked me to help create a global forum of survivors from across the planet.

Soon, survivors who had found their voice flew thousands of miles to come together and we discussed what needed to change in order to stop children being sexually exploited in the future. Everyone there, from every corner of the world, had suffered sexual violence in their childhood too, just like you.

It was never my goal to become an activist, I just kept taking the next natural step. I wrote the play to help my brothers. Then, when I realised it could help other people, I wanted to share it as widely as possible. Then, when I heard about all these people who couldn't even press charges because of some crazy old law in their country, I felt I had to do what I could to help them too. Eventually I found myself at the UN, chairing all these global discussions, the outcomes of which could eventually help billions of people. You don't have to do this though; you don't have to devote your life to saving others just because you have been abused. You can if you truly want to, but right now, just focus on saving your own life, like on an aeroplane when they say put on your own oxygen mask before helping someone put on theirs.

I was recently asked to give a talk in a high school and on the train there I got chatting with a nice lady next to me. She asked about my job and I said I'm actor and writer, and I'm also an activist.

She asked what an activist does and I had to think about it. Then I said,

"I do what I can to make the world better."

"Cool," she said. "But how?"

"Well, in various ways," I replied. "Sometimes by speaking at the UN or to various governments. Sometimes talking on TV or to groups of people. It depends what I'm trying to change."

She looked kind of sad and said, "Oh, I'm just a hairdresser."

I didn't like her response because hairdressing is awesome.

I told her, "Never say you are 'just' a hairdresser. You get people ready for their wedding or make them feel smart for a job interview. You make people feel beautiful on the most significant days of their lives. That is such an awesome job! The whole world needs its hair cut sometimes."

We all play our part. Whatever you want to do with your life, you can, but do it to the best of your ability. The world needs you to be *you*, as fully as you can be. I find that some people who have been abused use it as their excuse for not living the rest of their life. They turn their back on the world and say, "Why should I care? I've been hurt!"

Choosing to live this way will not lead you back to happiness. Some people who have been abused, however, use it as their reason to fully live the rest of their life. They turn towards the world and say, "I understand your pain because I have been hurt too."

A child who wrote to me recently made me realise that while I love encouraging positive change on an international level, the things I learned on my healing journey over the past twenty years could help you make some positive change in your life right now, so I wrote it all down for you. You have now discovered that the most important truth is:

**You are awesome and the world needs you.**

**Take one nice slow deep cleansing breath.**

**Imagine some time in your future when all this is behind you and you are completely happy.**

**What do you see?**

**Where are you?**

**Who else is with you?**

**Feel the relief and joy of this future moment.**

**It's not a dream. It will happen.**

**Try to visit this feeling every day until you are there.**

**Be proud of yourself. You're nailing it!**

# You have just completed Phase 1

**WELL DONE YOU!**

It might seem like the truth is just a bunch of nice ideas but it's because it is so simple that it is so hard to believe. The truth is:

**It's not fair.**

**There is nothing you could have done to stop what they did to you.**

**You have done nothing wrong. They did.**

**None of this is your fault.**

**Talking about it helps.**

**It's okay to not be okay.**

**Your whole life is not ruined.**

**You will be stronger because of what you have lived through.**

**You have nothing to be ashamed of, they have.**

**You are awesome and the world needs you.**

**Sorry, more breathing required.**

**Take three more breaths, for old time's sake.**

## Phase 2: Understanding

# The Truth

If you've understood everything I've already shared here, then congratulations, you have completed Phase 2. You are well on the road to recovery. If not, don't worry, you'll get there.

Look back over the ten truths in this little book. Underline the ones that make most sense to you. Circle the ones that don't, then discuss them with someone you trust.

If you really don't want to share anything with anyone in your life yet, you can find safe people to talk to online. There are some useful contacts at the back of this book that can help you find the right person to guide you through the next phase of your healing. Understanding the truth about what you have experienced is a great accomplishment. Many people who have been abused never achieve this.

You have done so well coming this far, but the real freedom is in what you do next.

Keep going.

You're going to be okay.

Phase 3: Believing

# The Truth

Healing is complete when we reach *Phase 3 – Believing the Truth*. This takes as long as it takes.

Understanding happens in your head, but believing happens in your heart. When you accept the truth in your heart and you finally know it, with every fibre of your being, you will be truly free from everything they did to you.

The therapeutic journey towards believing is through your emotions.

Sometimes real life is simply too sore. We automatically try to protect ourselves from the pain. To survive horrible experiences most of us instantly suppress our emotions. We hide all our fear, anger and sadness deep inside to stop ourselves from feeling them, but later when the danger has passed those strong emotions are still trapped inside us. To move on fully, we need to carefully let them out, so that we can finally let them go.

It's best if someone who is trained in supporting people through their healing is there to guide you in this process.

You don't need to start talking to someone about any of this until you are ready. Just remember that the sooner you start, the sooner you'll be okay.

If you try to be stone, like I did for so long, never letting yourself feel anything, you're just keeping yourself stuck. The heaviness of what you went through stays until you are ready to let it out, but once you do, you will literally feel lighter.

Do you ever feel bad or low, but you can't explain exactly why? Emotions are kind of like a phone that keeps ringing inside you. It won't stop until you answer it. It's annoying, you can't feel truly at peace with all that noise, but it's actually your heart that's calling, trying to get your attention. The easiest way to make it stop is to simply listen to what your heart is calling to say. Let yourself feel. Many of us were actually taught never to express emotion, so we prefer to be alone if we're feeling anything. That's the same across the world.

In that remote hotel in Norway, with forty other grown men from different countries who had all been abused in our childhood, we hung up a punch bag and hit it hard with a baseball bat to connect with our buried emotions and let them out. This was a safe place, so we screamed and shouted and cried and then laughed in relief as the great weight of all that pain was finally released.

That might sound weird or stupid, but it was worth it. These are practical steps that make a big difference in your ability to take back your life.

If you're too scared to show emotion in front of someone, you can wait until nobody's home and scream into your mattress. If you feel sad, put on a nice, cosy hoody, play some sad music, take deep breaths and breathe out slowly until you begin to cry. Remember, you won't cry forever and it's our body's natural way of releasing sadness. Once we let it all go, it's gone.

It's okay to want to be alone when you first start healing, if it makes you feel safer, but honestly, it's not good to isolate yourself for too long. Recovering from this stuff happens when you connect with safe people. You can't really hug yourself; you need someone else there.

See the back of this book for information on how to find safe people to help you reach Phase 3.

You truly are going to be okay.

If you are one of the many children whose own parent abused you, then imagine someone else who cares about you as you read this next page.

When I first started therapy in Wolverhampton, I was surprised to discover that I was angry with my mum for not protecting me. She used to make me say prayers and I would always ask why. She'd just say, "To keep you safe."

But I knew I wasn't safe the whole time. This made me so angry, but by talking about all this in therapy I realised that what her brother did was not her fault. She didn't know he was doing it. She would have stopped it if she had.

When I finally told the police, my mum found it too hard to talk to me about it all because she was so sad it had happened to her little child. She felt so guilty she'd let me down. She was heartbroken.

Even though it would have been uncomfortable, I wish I'd talked to her when I had the chance, but my mum died very suddenly. Now I can't say all the things to her I wish I had.

Talk to your parents or guardians, the people you know care for you. Say everything on your mind and in your heart. Remember they love you and they are so sad that someone did this to you. Even if they can't say it, they feel bad that they let you down.

**Last one, I promise... and breathe...**

# Epilogue

Phase 4: Living

# The Truth

The child who wrote me that letter asked if I think about the abuse a lot today. I've travelled all over the world speaking to governments and the media about abuse. Only because I chose this job do I think about my abuse often, but the memories do not affect how I feel anymore.

Even after the abuse stopped, there were times in my teens when I just wanted to give up. I'm so relieved that I decided to search for the truth. Even though it took me so long to find it, I'm so glad I went through the healing because my life is amazing now. When I was younger, I never imagined it could be this wonderful.

Remember, what you have been through might leave you believing that all adults are bad, but that's not true. You'll be one yourself one day, and you'll still be awesome. Many adults work so hard to stop these things ever happening to children. If no one has ever apologised to you for what that person did to you, then know that there are many, many good adults out there who are so sorry that this happened to you.

We are so sorry that we weren't there to protect you. We are so sorry that we didn't stop what they did to you. We are so sorry.

It was done to many of us too and we understand how you feel.

I don't imagine I'll ever meet you, but I am so proud of you. I wrote this book for you because I want you to take your life back. Don't ever let them win.

You are going to be okay, even if you cannot see how right now. You are stronger than you know. You have your whole life ahead of you and you can make it anything you want it to be.

You deserve it.

**Remember the joy and relief you will feel when this is all behind you.**

**Hold on to that feeling.**

# Help

For information on where to find confidential help near you, wherever you are in the world, visit:

www.helpnearme.info

## Immediate help - UK and Ireland

To talk to someone right now, no matter where you live in the UK, phone Childline. They will connect you privately with a trained counsellor and everything you tell them is confidential. This call won't even appear on your phone bill. If you are in immediate danger, they will talk you through what to do next. Call 0800 1111 or chat to them via text at **www.childline.org.uk**

If you or someone you know is in immediate danger, you can call the police on 999 or, if you want to report something that happened recently, call 101.

You can find confidential support in your area, anywhere across the UK and Ireland.

Visit **www.thesurvivorstrust.org/find-support/**

Or you can contact The Moira Anderson Foundation for advice. Call 01236 602890 or visit **www.moiraanderson.org**

For information on where to find confidential help near you in other European countries, visit: **www.helpnearme.info**

## Immediate help - North America

To talk to someone right now, no matter where you live in the USA or Canada, call the National Child Abuse Hotline. They have interpreters for 170 languages who are available twenty-four hours a day, seven days a week. All calls are confidential
(1-800) 422 4453

If you or someone you know is in immediate danger, call the police on 911.

You can find confidential support in your area, anywhere across the USA, visit **www.rainn.org** or **www.d2l.org**

For information on where to find confidential help near you, wherever you are in the world, visit: **www.helpnearme.info**

# Self-Help

Here are some practical, nonverbal self-help techniques that you can start using right now no matter where you live.

## Tapping

Tapping, also known as the Emotional Freedom Technique, is a simple and effective way of helping yourself to let go of any strong emotion. It's a powerful and natural way to instantly calm yourself down, anytime anywhere. You can learn the basic tapping sequence at:
**www.thetappingsolution.com**

## Havening

Havening is a newly developed technique which helps you to remove the emotional charge around traumatic memories. Using this process, you can stop yourself feeling overwhelmed. You don't lose the memories, but the memories can lose all negative effect on you today. Go to **www.havening.org** or search for video demonstrations by its creator, Dr Ronald A. Ruden

## Meditation:

You might think meditation is weird or boring or even spooky, but it's just exercise for your brain to help it become stronger. We are constantly told that we must exercise our bodies to stay healthy and strong, but meditating regularly helps keep our mind healthy and strong. Surely that's even more important.

Here are three types of meditation that I've learned and can highly recommend:

### Mindfulness Meditation

"Headspace" is excellent for beginners. This smartphone app has a free ten-day trial and is the perfect introduction to "Mindfulness". You just sit quietly wearing headphones for ten minutes and it guides you through a simple relaxing meditation, so your mind can get some rest from the usual thoughts that fill your head all day.
**www.headspace.com**

### Transcendental Meditation (TM)

This is a very powerful technique that puts your mind and body into a state of deep rest, normally for about twenty minutes every morning. It's now recommended to soldiers returning from war and people who've survived car accidents because TM allows your mind and body the space it needs to heal itself. In time, a cut on your arm heals up if you just leave it alone. Your mind will also return to health if you give it the proper time and space it needs to heal, and TM is that time and space. It takes a weekend to learn how to practice TM properly and

"The Meditation Trust" is a UK charity that offers courses at a discounted rate. There are others around the world.
UK: **www.meditationtrust.com**
USA: **www.tm.org**
Rest of the world: **www.tm.org/choose-your-country**

## Vipassanna

This is the most powerful meditation technique that exists. It was created in India over 2500 years ago, like yoga but for your mind. Like yoga, it is not religious or spiritual. Anyone can learn Vipassanna and anyone who practices it regularly develops a permanent state of peace and happiness. It helps you let go of the past and strengthens you to deal with anything in the future, which is why Vipassanna is described as "The art of living". All courses are free but are run on donations from past students. I highly recommend the ten-day course but there are shorter weekend courses for young people and beginners.
**www.dhamma.org**

## Alternative Therapies:

### Laughter Therapy

Possibly the strangest but most fun process I've ever experienced. Laughter Therapy pretty much involves just laughing, but not at anything in particular. At first you might feel a bit self-conscious, but once you've tried this, you will recommend it. It floods your body with natural happiness and reduces stress.

See a demonstration of a laughter wellness session at www.laughteronlineuniversity.com or visit **www.laughtertherapy.org.uk**

### Transformational breath work

Sometimes our bodies store traumatic experiences by holding onto tension. Breath work gently helps you release any lingering stress, without even needing to talk about what caused it. Learn more at: **www.breathingtree.co.uk** or **www.thebreathingroom.co.uk**

**And… relax.**

**I wish you Peace**

**and**

**Happiness.**

**Peace and Happiness do not come from just hoping**

**that life will be filled with only good times,**

**because** *no one's is.*

**Peace and Happiness come from understanding**

**that life is filled with both good and hard times,**

**but knowing that whatever happens,**

**you'll be okay.**

**The Truth is,**

**in case no one who really understands**

**what you're going through has ever told you,**

**you *are* going to be okay.**